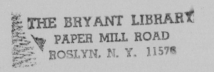

The Secretive Timber Rattlesnake

text and photographs by
BIANCA LAVIES

DUTTON CHILDREN'S BOOKS
New York

ACKNOWLEDGMENTS

for sharing time, knowledge, and thoughts:

Richard M. Meszler, Ph.D., Department of Anatomy,
    Baltimore College of Dental Surgery,
    University of Maryland at Baltimore
John L. Behler, Department of Herpetology, New York
    Zoological Society
Laurie Bingaman and Michael Davenport, Department of
    Herpetology, National Zoological Park
Dr. William S. Brown and Betsy Franz, Skidmore College
Bruce Shwedick, Reptile World, Inc.
Mary Smith and Nelson Brown, *National Geographic*
Randy Stechert, research assistant

Library of Congress Cataloging-in-Publication Data

Lavies, Bianca.
    The secretive timber rattlesnake/text and photographs by
Bianca Lavies.—1st ed.
        p. cm.
    Summary: Describes the physical characteristics, behavior,
and life cycle of the timid but venomous timber rattlesnake.
    ISBN 0-525-44572-2
    1. Timber rattlesnake—Juvenile literature.   [1. Timber
rattlesnake.   2. Snakes.]   I. Title.   90-31964
QL666.069L38   1990   CIP
597.96—dc20   AC

Published in the United States by Dutton Children's Books,
a division of Penguin Books USA Inc.

Designer: Kathleen Westray

Printed in Hong Kong
First Edition   10 9 8 7 6 5 4 3 2 1

To the memory of my little friend Bonnie Brown,
who wanted to be a photographer too,
and to the memory of Alfie, her cat

Imagine that you are walking in the mountains of the eastern United States. Suddenly you hear a buzzing noise. It's similar to the whirring sound of a cicada. But it is really the sound of a timber rattlesnake, shaking the rattlelike end of its tail to warn you to keep your distance.

Otherwise, you might not notice the timber rattlesnake, which tends to stay quietly out of sight. The timber rattler is not an

aggressive creature. Unlike some of its more combative cousins, such as prairie and western diamondback rattlesnakes, it is a secretive snake and will usually slither away when threatened. But beware, because like all rattlers, the timber rattlesnake has a venomous bite. It will use its venom to protect itself, but mostly to kill its prey in order to eat, grow, and reproduce.

The timber rattler's coloring blends in with its surroundings and hides the snake from animals that might eat it, such as raccoons and hawks. Its body is covered with tough scales that are flexible like our fingernails but much thinner. The scales are dry, not slimy, and they overlap like shingles on a roof.

This female timber rattlesnake will soon give birth to baby rattlers. She mated with a male last fall, just over a year ago, and stored his sperm in her body. In June, her eggs were ready to be fertilized by the sperm, and the baby rattlesnakes began to grow in egg sacs inside of her.

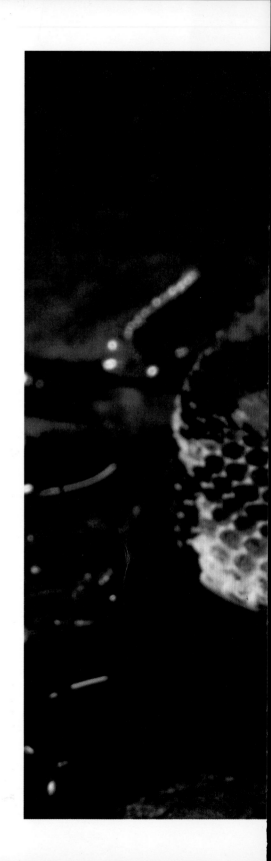

In September, the mother timber rattlesnake gives birth to nine babies, each between ten and thirteen inches long. As the baby rattlers squeeze out of their mother's body, their egg sacs break. These babies are so well-nourished from the yolks in the sacs that they will not need a meal until the spring. But even without eating, they begin to grow —and grow fast.

Ten days later, this baby's muscular body is already developing, and the young snake will shed its scaly skin for the first time.

A few days before shedding, the snake's glands produced a milky substance between the old skin and the new one. This moist substance, which dulls the snake's coloring, will help the old skin peel off easily.

The young rattler rubs its head against a rock until the skin around its mouth splits and starts to peel back. As it rubs its body hard against the ground, the skin rolls back like a sock. Finally, the old skin peels off completely and is left behind, inside out. For the rest of its life, the timber rattlesnake will continue to grow and will shed its skin this way, one to three times a year.

Now that the snake *(below, left)* has finished shedding, it looks brighter and shinier than the two on the right. But soon these snakes will shed too and reveal gleaming new skins.

Also visible when the baby rattler first sheds is a hard nub, or button, at the end of its body. This button, which you can see on the snake at the left, is the beginning of its rattle.

The rattle develops piece by piece. The next time the snake sheds, the skin covering the very tip of its body will loosen. It will become dry and brittle, but will not be shed. Hollow and hard like a shell, this section of skin stays attached to the snake, forming the next segment of its rattle. At each shedding, another interlocking segment is added.

Someday this baby snake may have as large a rattle as its mother's, shown here. The button is missing from her rattle, and other pieces may have broken off too, caught between rocks or fallen branches. But by counting the segments, you can estimate how often this mother snake has shed. Her rattle has eleven pieces and once had a button, so she has shed at least twelve times.

When a rattlesnake is alarmed, it shakes its tail very fast. The segments of its rattle vibrate against each other, making the buzzing noise that warns other creatures to stay away—or risk a venomous bite.

Rattlesnakes are reptiles, and like all reptiles, their body temperatures change with the temperature of the environment. As the weather grows colder, the young timber rattlers can tell instinctively that they must find a place to keep warm. Their mother has already gone to seek shelter for the coming winter.

A timber rattlesnake has two nostrils. But it also has a remarkable sense organ in the roof of its mouth that tells the snake more than its sense of smell alone can. When a timber rattler flicks its delicate forked tongue in and out, it picks up tiny molecules from the air and ground. Then the snake lifts its tongue to the organ in its mouth, called Jacobson's organ, which helps identify the molecules and the creatures they came from.

It is believed that by using Jacobson's organ, the baby snakes can find—and follow—a trail left by adult snakes leading to their winter den.

Baby rattlesnakes may freeze to death if the temperature suddenly drops before they can reach shelter. But this young timber rattler has found its way in time to the family den, almost hidden from sight.

An older, larger rattlesnake lies curled at the entrance. Other timber rattlers, including the baby rattler's mother, have already taken refuge inside the rocky cave. It has probably been used by the baby snake's ancestors for hundreds of years. Autumn after autumn, for as long as they live, these rattlesnakes will come back to this den when the weather turns cold.

By the middle of October, dozens of timber rattlesnakes are inside the low, dark cave. But this photographer can see only one of them. Most have disappeared into secret cracks and crevices. The snake in the picture below will soon crawl out of sight too.

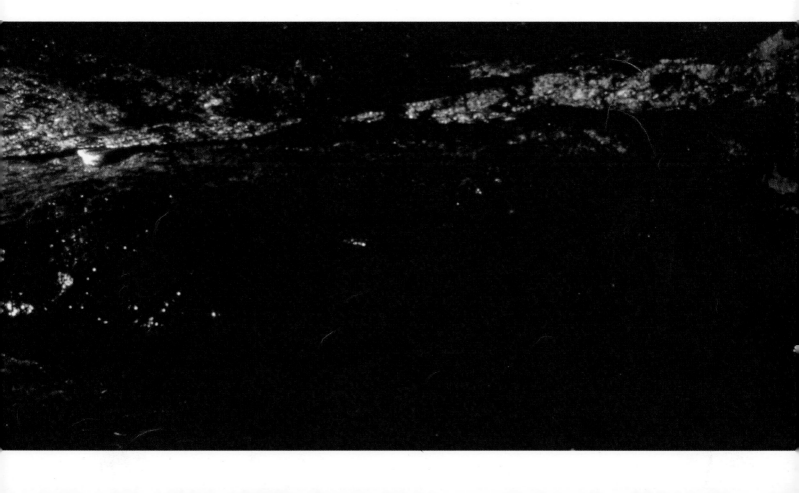

In their hiding places deep inside the cave, the snakes will be protected from the bitter cold and frost. They will not freeze. But it will get cold enough in the cave that their temperatures will drop. As the snakes grow colder, their body functions will slow down.

All winter long, the snakes lie there, using only enough energy to breathe and to keep their hearts beating and blood circulating. The hibernating snakes do not need food or water until spring.

As spring approaches, the days grow longer, and
the weather grows warmer. In April, the snakes begin
to stir, and soon they emerge from their hiding

places and move closer to the cave's entrance.
Their body temperatures rise with the temperature
of the cave, and they become more active.

When the weather is warm enough, timber rattlesnakes slither out of their family den, hungry and thirsty. Their senses guide them to water. And with the help of their tongues and Jacobson's organs, timber rattlers can pick up the fresh trails of mice or chipmunks and track them to their burrows.

A mouse foraging near its burrow may not see the well-camouflaged timber rattlesnake. But even in the dark, the rattler can tell when a mouse is close by. On each side of the snake's head, near each nostril, is a pitlike opening. The nerve endings inside these pits are sensitive to heat and can detect a warm-blooded animal several feet away. This female timber rattlesnake will curl up, motionless, and wait. And when a mouse comes close ...

3.

The rattlesnake strikes. Her jaws open wide, and her two fangs, covered by pink, gumlike sheaths, swing forward as if on hinges. As she stabs the mouse with her fangs, muscles around her poison glands contract, squeezing venom through the hollow fangs and into the mouse's body.

Then the snake releases the mouse. The mouse stumbles away, but it does not get far. The snake's venom kills it in a matter of minutes.

The timber rattler trails her prey and nudges it to make sure it is dead.

Not until the mouse is dead will the rattlesnake eat it. Her flexible jaws open wide as she works first one side of her mouth and then the other over the mouse's head. Her fangs and her sharp, backward-pointing teeth are used not to chew, but to pull the mouse inside her mouth.

Once the timber rattler has completely swallowed the mouse, both of her sheathed fangs will swing back up toward the roof of her mouth until they are needed again. Fangs break off or fall out several times a year and are replaced by new ones.

Muscle contractions move the mouse from the snake's mouth through the esophagus and into the stomach. The powerful venom that killed the mouse also helps to break it down, even before it reaches the snake's digestive system. It may take as long as four days for the rattler to digest this mouse.

A timber rattlesnake may eat twenty or more meals a year, or as few as six, depending on how much food is available when the snake is hungry.

Hunting for food and water, slithering unseen between rocks and plants, lying in the sun to keep warm, hibernating in a hidden cave in winter, the timber rattlesnake leads a slow, quiet, secretive life. Some timber rattlers live as long as fifteen years and may grow to six feet. But most timber rattlesnakes die before reaching full growth. Some are killed by natural predators, but most are killed by people encroaching upon the snakes' environment.

In some states, timber rattlers are now protected by law. They play an important role in nature's balance, as they help control the population of mice and other rodents. And though they are retiring and nonaggressive, they should be avoided like any venomous snake and certainly not provoked.

So the next time you walk in the eastern mountains or forests and hear a rattling sound, look to see if you have stepped into a timber rattlesnake's secret world. Then quickly step out of its way, and let it go in peace.

When Bianca Lavies went back to the timber rattlesnakes' den in early spring, she knew that to photograph them, she would again have to slide like a snake over the cold, damp cave floor. She also knew that the rattlers were probably starting to stir, and after storing up venom all winter long, their bite would be especially dangerous.

"Some rattlers lay quietly curled on a ledge," says Bianca. "They looked at me and then very slowly moved away into the depths of the cave, too shallow for me to follow.

"One timber rattlesnake stayed behind. We faced each other. I knew that if it decided to come toward me, I couldn't move away fast enough because I was tightly wedged between the top and bottom of the cave. I kept breathing very deeply and slowly to stay relaxed.

"If I am relaxed, I thought, the snake will feel that and will relax too. If I send it messages that my visit is a friendly one, the snake will feel better about my being here.

"So I did. For three-quarters of an hour, we eyed each other. I took some pictures. Then I inched backward, toward my own world, with the happy feeling that perhaps I had made another animal friend."